SELECTED POEMS

ALINE KILMER

ESSAYS

HUNTING A HAIR SHIRT AND OTHER SPIRITUAL ADVENTURES

POEMS

THE POOR KING'S DAUGHTER

VIGILS

CANDLES THAT BURN

SELECTED POEMS

JUVENILES

EMMY, NICKY AND GREG

TO BUTTONWOOD AND BACK

SELECTED POEMS

BY

ALINE KILMER

1929

DOUBLEDAY, DORAN & COMPANY, INC.

GARDEN CITY, N. Y.

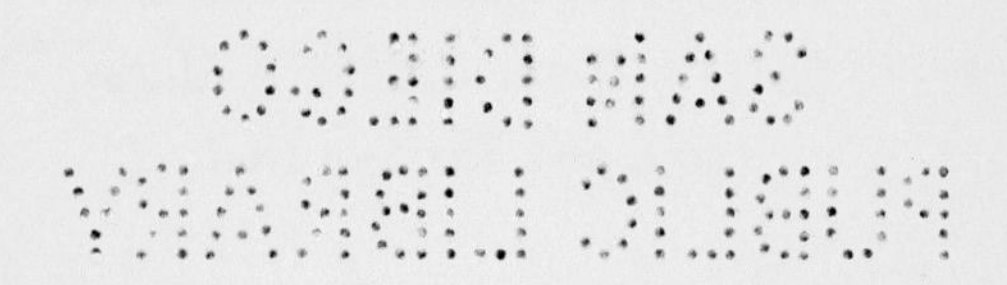

PRINTED IN THE UNITED STATES AT
THE COUNTRY LIFE PRESS
GARDEN CITY, N. Y.

FIRST EDITION

ACKNOWLEDGMENTS

For permission to reprint the poems in this book, I thank the editors of *America*, *The Bookman*, *The Commonweal*, *The Delineator*, *Good Housekeeping*, *Harper's Magazine*, *Hearst's International*, *The Lyric*, *The Outlook*, *Poetry: A Magazine of Verse*, *The Queen's Work*, *Scribner's Magazine*, and *The Sun Dial*.

CONTENTS

PART ONE

PART TWO

PART THREE

PART ONE

AGAINST THE WALL

If I live till my fighting days are done
I must fasten my armour on my eldest son.

I would give him better, but this is my best.
I can get along without it—I'll be glad to have a rest.

And I'll sit mending armour with my back against the
wall,
Because I have a second son, if this one should fall.

So I'll make it very shiny and I'll whistle very loud,
And I'll clap him on the shoulder and I'll say, very
proud:

"This is the lance *I* used to bear!"
But I mustn't tell what happened when I bore it.
"This is the helmet *I* used to wear!"
But I won't say what befell me when I wore it.

For you couldn't tell a youngster, it wouldn't be right,
That you wish you had died in your very first fight.

And I mustn't say that victory is never worth the cost,
That defeat may be bitter, but it's better to have lost.

And I mustn't say that glory is as barren as a stone.
I'd better not say anything, but leave the lad alone.

So he'll fight very bravely and probably he'll fall:
And I'll sit mending armour with my back against the
wall.

TRIBUTE

Deborah and Christopher brought me dandelions,
Kenton brought me buttercups with summer on their breath,
But Michael brought an autumn leaf, a lacy filigree,
A wan leaf, a ghost leaf, beautiful as death.

Death in all loveliness, fragile and exquisite,
Who but he would choose it from all the blossoming land?
Who but he would find it where it hid among the flowers?
Death in all loveliness, he laid it in my hand.

WILL-O'-THE-WISP

Your mother's bitterness, your father's woe,
By alchemy of love and piteous laughter,
Gave you your elfin grace
And a lost angel's face:
I dare not think what may become of you hereafter.

There is no peace for you that I can see;
Will-o'-the-wisp, swayed beyond will and reason:
Holding my breath for fear—
O dangerously dear!—
I shall delight in you for this brief season.

PREVISION

I know you are too dear to stay;
You are so exquisitely sweet:
My lonely house will thrill some day
To echoes of your eager feet.

I hold your words within my heart,
So few, so infinitely dear;
Watching your fluttering hands I start
At the corroding touch of fear.

A faint, unearthly music rings
From you to Heaven—it is not far!
A mist about your beauty clings
Like a thin cloud before a star.

My heart shall keep the child I knew,
When you are really gone from me,
And spend its life remembering you
As shells remember the lost sea.

"A WIND IN THE NIGHT"

A wind rose in the night,
  (She had always feared it so!)
Sorrow plucked at my heart
  And I could not but go.

Softly I went and stood
  By her door at the end of the hall.
Dazed with grief I watched
  The candles flaring and tall.

The wind was wailing aloud:
  I thought how she would have cried
For my warm familiar arms
  And the sense of me by her side.

The candles flickered and leapt,
  The shadows jumped on the wall.
She lay before me small and still
  And did not care at all.

AFTER GRIEVING

When I was young I was so sad!
  I was so sad! I did not know
Why any living thing was glad
  When one must some day sorrow so.
    But now that grief has come to me
    My heart is like a bird set free.

I always knew that it would come;
  I always felt it waiting there:
Its shadow kept my glad voice dumb
  And crushed my gay soul with despair.
    But now that I have lived with grief
    I feel an exquisite relief.

Runners who knew their proven strength,
  Ships that have shamed the hurricane:
These are my brothers, and at length
  I shall come back to joy again.
    However hard my life may be
    I know it shall not conquer me.

PART TWO

I SHALL NOT BE AFRAID

I shall not be afraid any more,
  Either by night or day;
What would it profit me to be afraid
  With you away?

Now I am brave. In the dark night alone
  All through the house I go,
Locking the doors and making windows fast
  When sharp winds blow.

For there is only sorrow in my heart;
  There is no room for fear.
But how I wish I were afraid again,
  My dear, my dear!

IF I HAD LOVED YOU MORE

If I had loved you more God would have had pity;
He would never have left me here in this desolate place,
Left me to go on my knees to the door of Heaven
Crying in vain for a little sight of your face.

How could I know that the earth would be dark without you?
For you were always the lover and I the friend.
Now if there were any hope that I might find you
I would go seeking you to the world's end.

"God is a jealous God. You have loved too wildly,
You have loved too well!" one said.
I bowed my head, but my heart in scorn was crying
That you whom I had not loved enough are dead.

I look on my heart and see it is hard and narrow,
That my loves are slight and last but a little space.
But why do I go on my knees to the door of Heaven
Crying for only a little sight of your face?

ATONEMENT

When a storm comes up at night and the wind is crying,
When the trees are moaning like masts on labouring ships,
I wake in fear and put out my hand to find you,
With your name on my lips.

No pain that the heart can hold is like to this one—
To call, forgetting, into aching space,
To reach out confident hands and find beside you
Only an empty place.

This should atone for the hours when I forget you.
Take them my offering, clean and sharp and sweet,
An agony brighter than years of dull remembrance.
I lay it at your feet.

THE NIGHT COMETH

My garden walks were smooth and green
  And edged with box trees left and right,
An old grey sun-dial stood between
  Two rounded bee hives, low and white.
My hollyhocks grew tall and red,
  My larkspur thrust its lances high:
"The Night Cometh," the sun-dial said,
  And I hated its wisdom and hurried by.

I watch the sun-dial as I wait
  And hope to see its slow hand fly.
The stately poplars at the gate
  Are funeral torches flaring high.
The scent of wallflowers breaks my heart,
  The box is bitter in the sun,
The poppies burst their sheathes apart
  And tell of rest when pain is done.

The hawthorn shakes a ghostly head
  And breathes of death at fullest noon.
"The Night Cometh," the sun-dial said—

The night can never come too soon.
O sun-dial, hurry your creeping hand,
Let the shadows fall where the brown bees hum,
I watch and wait where the low hives stand,
Let the night come, let the night come!

MOONLIGHT

The moon reached in cold hands across the sill
  And touched me as I lay sleeping;
And in my sleep I thought of sorrowful things:
  I wakened, and I lay weeping.

I could hear on the beach below the small waves break
  And fall on the silver shingle,
And the sound of a footstep passing in the street
  Where lamplight and moonlight mingle.

And I said: "All day I can turn my face to the sun
  And lead my thoughts to laughter;
But I hope in my heart that I never shall sleep again
  Because of the pain thereafter."

The moon's pale fingers wandered across my face
  And the arm where my hot cheek rested,
And because of the tears in my eyes I could not see
  Where the black waves rocked moon-crested.

THE GARDEN

And now it is all to be done over again,
  And what will come of it only God can know.
What has become of the furrows ploughed by pain,
  And the plants set row on row?

Where are the lines of beautiful bending trees,
  The gracious springs, the depths of delicate shade,
The sunny spaces loud with the humming of bees,
  And the grassy paths in the garden my life had made?

Lightning and earthquake now have blasted and riven;
  Even the trees that I trusted could not stand:
Now it lies here to the bitter winds of heaven—
  A barren and a desolated land.

MY MIRROR

There is a mirror in my room
Less like a mirror than a tomb,
There are so many ghosts that pass
Across the surface of the glass.

When in the morning I arise
With circles round my tired eyes,
Seeking the glass to brush my hair
My mother's mother meets me there.

If in the middle of the day
I happen to go by that way,
I see a smile I used to know—
My mother, twenty years ago.

But when I rise by candlelight
To feed my baby in the night,
Then whitely in the glass I see
My dead child's face look out at me.

THINGS

Sometimes when I am at tea with you
I catch my breath
At a thought that is old as the world is old,
And more bitter than death.

It is that the spoon that you just laid down
And the cup that you hold
May be here shining and insolent
When you are still and cold.

Your careless note that I laid away
May leap to my eyes like flame
When the world has almost forgotten your voice
Or the sound of your name.

The golden Virgin da Vinci drew
May smile on over my head,
And daffodils nod in the silver vase
When you are dead.

So let moth and rust corrupt and thieves
Break through and I shall be glad,

Because of the hatred I bear to things
Instead of the love I had.

For life seems only a shuddering breath,
A smothered, desperate cry,
And things have a terrible permanence
When people die.

KNOWLEDGE

Some learn it in their youth,
  Some after bitter years:
There is no escape from the truth
  Though we drown in our tears.

Many die when they see
  That the terrible thing is true.
But it has been easy for me:
  I always knew.

THE STIRRUP CUP

Here where each road-worn one
Rests till the night is done,
   In the grey dawning I saw my horse stand,
And as I left the inn
With his smooth face of sin
   Smiling, mine host with a cup in his hand.

"Drink now, my merry friend,
Drink to your journey's end.
   Let not the hour of our parting be sad.
Follow what road you will
One thought will cheer you still—
   This warm and fragrant cup you shall have had.

"Traveller, the ride is sweet,
God speed your flying feet,
   Thinking you hasten to lover and friend.
Gather the bridle up,
Drain dry the stirrup cup,
   Only a cup of tears waits at the end."

FAVETE LINGUIS

Speak not the word that turns the flower to ashes,
  Praise not the beauty passing as you gaze.
Let your eyes drink of loveliness in silence:
  It will but wither even as you praise.

See there the plum tree heavy with its blossom
  Swings like the full moon, glimmering and round:
You lift your lute to celebrate its beauty
  And all its petals flutter to the ground.

PART THREE

TO A LADY COMPLIMENTING

When I met you an hour ago
My heart was heavy and chill;
Now, from your word of praise,
It is glowing still.

Ah, *vanitas vanitatum!*
What the Preacher said was true!
I always thought my eyes were grey
But now I know they are blue.

PTOLEMAIC

When Ptolemy sat watching from his roof
The great stars moving through the purple night
He knew that they went swinging round the earth:
And I believe that Ptolemy was right.

I know the moon is but a silver disc
Blown across heaven. You see it blowing plainly.
I know the world has towering walls of brass
Round which the seas of all the earth beat vainly.

The heaven I know is a more decent cover
Than your infinitude of yawning space.
What have you gained by making things all over
Into a most intolerable place?

WARNING

O don't go out from your witch's house
Through the whippoorwill-haunted night!
How do you know you'll ever come back?
For the vine swings clutching across your feet,
The hands of the hedge reach out and out,
The arms of the trees sweep down and around,
And nobody'll know the way you went
When you never come home any more.

And don't come back to your witch's house
After the dark is down.
The shadows leap from your candle's flare
To swallow the corners up.
The curtain sways where no one passed,
The cat stands staring into the dark,
And God knows what may be sitting there
In the chair with its back to the door.

SONG AGAINST CHILDREN

O the barberry bright, the barberry bright!
It stood on the mantelpiece because of the height.
Its stems were slender and thorny and tall
And it looked most beautiful against the grey wall.
But Michael climbed up there in spite of the height
And he ate all the berries off the barberry bright.

O the round holly wreath, the round holly wreath!
It hung in the window with ivy beneath.
It was plump and prosperous, spangled with red,
And I thought it would cheer me although I were dead.
But Deborah climbed on a table beneath
And she ate all the berries off the round holly wreath.

O the mistletoe bough, the mistletoe bough!
Could anyone touch it? I did not see how.
I hung it up high that it might last long,
I wreathed it with ribbons and hailed it with song.
But Christopher reached it, I do not know how,
And he ate all the berries off the mistletoe bough.

FOR THE BIRTHDAY OF A MIDDLE-AGED CHILD

I'm sorry you are wiser,
  I'm sorry you are taller;
I liked you better foolish,
  And I liked you better smaller.
I'm sorry you have learning
  And I hope you won't display it;
But since this is your birthday
  I suppose I mustn't say it.

I liked you with your hair cut
  Like a mediæval page's,
And I hate to see your eyes change
  From a seraph's to a sage's.
You are not half so beautiful
  Since middle-age befell you;
But since this is your birthday
  I suppose I mustn't tell you.

JUSTICE

Michael, come in! Stop crying at the door.
  Come in and see the evil you have done.
  Here is your sister's doll with one leg gone,
Naked and helpless on the playroom floor.
"Poor child! poor child! now he can never stand.
  With one leg less he could not even sit!"
She mourned, but first, with swift avenging hand,
  She smote, and I am proud of her for it.

Michael, my sympathies are all for you.
  Your cherub mouth, your miserable eyes,
  Your grey-blue smock tear-spattered and your cries
Shatter my heart, but what am I to do?
He was her baby and the fear of bears
  Lay heavy on him so he could not sleep
But in the crook of her dear arm, she swears.
  So, Michael, she was right and you must weep.

THE TOUCH OF TEARS

Michael walks in autumn leaves,
  Rustling leaves and fading grasses,
And his little music-box
  Tinkles faintly as he passes.
It's a gay and jaunty tune,
  If the hands that play were clever:
Michael plays it like a dirge,
  Moaning on and on forever.

While his happy eyes grow big,
  Big and innocent and soulful,
Wistful, halting little notes
  Rise, unutterably doleful,
Telling of all childish griefs—
  Baffled babies sob forsaken,
Birds fly off and bubbles burst,
  Kittens sleep and will not waken.

Michael, it's the touch of tears.
  Though you sing for very gladness,

Others will not see your mirth;
  They will mourn your fancied sadness.
Though you laugh at them in scorn,
  Show your happy heart for token,
Michael, you'll protest in vain—
  They will swear your heart is broken!

EXPERIENCE

Deborah danced, when she was two,
As buttercups and daffodils do;
Spirited, frail, naïvely bold,
Her hair a ruffled crest of gold,
And whenever she spoke her voice went singing
Like water up from a fountain springing.

But now her step is quiet and slow;
She walks the way primroses go;
Her hair is yellow instead of gilt,
Her voice is losing its lovely lilt,
And in place of her wild, delightful ways
A quaint precision rules her days.

For Deborah now is three, and oh,
She knows so much that she did not know.

A DIDACTIC POEM TO DEBORAH

Deborah dear, when you are old,
  Tired and grey, with pallid brow,
Where will you put the blue and gold
  And radiant rose that tint you now?

You are so fair, so gay, so sweet!
  How can I bear to watch you grow,
Knowing that soon those twinkling feet
  Must go the ways all children go?

Deborah, put the blue and gold
  And rosy beauty that is you,
Into your heart that it may hold
  Beauty to last your whole life through.

Then, though the world be tossed and torn,
  Greyer than ashes and as sad,
Though fate may make your way forlorn,
  Deborah dear, you shall be glad.

CANDLES THAT BURN

Candles that burn for a November birthday,
  Wreathed round with asters and with goldenrod,
As you go upward in your radiant dying
  Carry my prayer to God.

Tell Him she is so small and so rebellious,
  Tell Him her words are music on her lips,
Tell Him I love her in her wayward beauty
  Down to her fingertips.

Ask Him to keep her brave and true and lovely,
  Vivid and happy, gay as she is now,
Ask Him to let no shadow touch her beauty,
  No sorrow mar her brow.

All the sweet saints that came for her baptising,
  Tell them I pray them to be always near.
Ask them to keep her little feet from stumbling,
  Her gallant heart from fear.

Candles that burn for a November birthday,
  Wreathed round with asters and with goldenrod,
As you go upward in your radiant dying,
  Carry my prayer to God.

PART FOUR

see p. 25

SHARDS

I can never remake the thing I have destroyed;
I brushed the golden dust from the moth's bright wing,
I called down wind to shatter the cherry-blossoms,
I did a terrible thing.

I feared that the cup might fall, so I flung it from me;
I feared that the bird might fly, so I set it free;
I feared that the dam might break, so I loosed the river:
May its waters cover me.

YOU ASK ME NOT TO DIE

You need not fear;
You need not dread that day I shall be dying:
I shall not leave you, dear.
Others more tender, with more hope than I,
Lift thrush-sweet voices, lyrically crying
That they are soon to die.
But I shall live to see each starry head
That I have loved go down to its low bed,
And I shall wander through a ruined land
Where there will be no dear, accustomed hand
To ease my sorrow.
Nay, Sweet, to-morrow
Your flower-like beauty may have failed and fled,
And I shall weep you dead;
Then rise to face the grim and hooded years,
Each with his vase of tears,
That move majestically by;
Till the little I had of beauty will be but a withered mask,
And the little I had of wit will be bitter and dry.
Dear, you do not know what it is that you ask,
How can you love me and bid me not to die?

COMPLAINT

I could have lived content in a snail's shell.
What tore me forth and furnished me with wings,
And set me here with other tortured things
Beating a painful way to Heaven or Hell?
  Why could I not be left to creep and die?
  I watch my wings with vague reproachful eye—
  I never wished to fly.

SONG

Love goes
As the wind blows,
And no man knows
  The place thereof.
But Pity stays
Through weary days
  Keeping the house of Love.

Though you come late
To the swinging gate,
The path is straight
  And the door is wide,
And Pity's eyes
Are so sadly wise
  You will think it is Love inside.

TO APHRODITE: WITH A MIRROR

Here, Cyprian, is my jewelled looking-glass,
My final gift to bind my final vow:
I cannot see myself as I once was;
I would not see myself as I am now.

CHARMIAN'S SONG

I'm glad I have but a little heart—
For my heart is very small—
It makes it free to come and go
And no one cares at all.

I give my heart for a tender word,
For a gentle look or touch,
And the one who has it never knows
And it does not hurt me much.

If my heart were great and I gave it away
Then all the world would see,
But my heart is only a little thing
And it does not trouble me.

I may give my little heart unseen,
It is so small and light,
And only very wakeful things
Can hear it cry at night.

PERVERSITY

All my life I have loved where I was not loved,
  And always those whom I did not love loved me;
Only the God who made my wild heart knows
  Why this should be.

Oh, you are strange, inscrutable and proud;
  I cannot prove you though I try and try.
You'll keep my love alive and wondering
  Until I die.

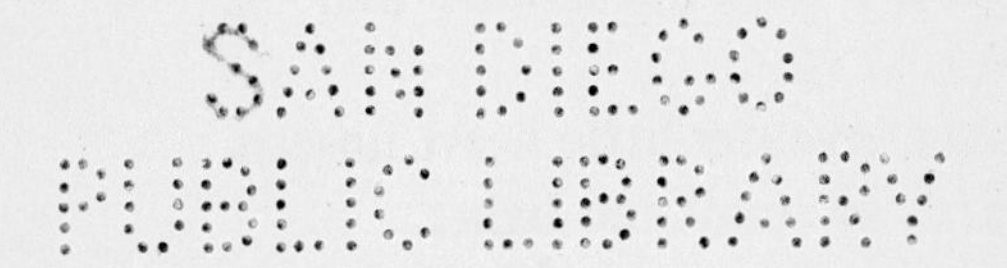

"THE HEART KNOWETH ITS OWN BITTERNESS"

The heart knoweth? If this be true indeed
Then the thing that I bear in my bosom is not a heart;
For it knows no more than a hollow, whispering reed
That answers to every wind.
I am sick of the thing! I think we had better part.

My heart will come to any piper's calling,
A fool in motley that dances for any king;
But my body knows, and its tears unbidden falling
Say that my heart has sinned.
You would have my heart? You may. I am sick of the thing.

The web flew out and floated wide.
  Poor lady! I was with her then.
She gathered up her piteous pride,
  But she could never weave again.

The mirror cracked from side to side;
  I saw its silver shadows go.
"The curse has come on me!" she cried.
  Poor lady! I had told her so.

She was so proud: she would not hide.
  She only laughed and tried to sing.
But singing, in her song she died.
  She did not profit anything.

TOUR DE FORCE

Smilingly, out of my pain,
  I have woven a little song;
    You may take it away with you.
I shall not sing it again,
    But when you have learned it through
  It will keep you brave and strong.
I wove it out of my pain:
    There is not a word of it true.

TO SAPPHO: ABOUT HER APPLE

The highest apple swinging in the treetop
Fell in my two hands, eagerly uplifted.
For though I knew its height was half its fairness,
    Still I would have it.

Now I am wise with centuries of wisdom.
I lift my voice to give your ashes comfort:
Sappho, the tempting fruit that hung above you
    Was hard and bitter.

ESCAPE

Indifference may snare me, but only devotion can hold
me:
Where is the net you spread in hope that its meshes
might fold me?
Like a shadow I slipped through a web too slight to
bind me;
Now free and wise I cast the last frail threads on the
wind behind me.

BOUND

If I had loved you, soon, ah, soon I had lost you.
Had I been kind you had kissed me and gone your faithless way.
The kiss that I would not give is the kiss that your lips are holding:
Now you are mine forever, because of all I have cost you.

You think that you are free and have given over your sighing,
You think that from my coldness your love has flown away:
But mine are the hands you shall dream that your own are holding,
And mine is the face you shall look for when you are dying.

REFUGE

I am glad I have come.
Let me stay;
I would not go home.
Let me rest in your kindness,
Your blessed blindness,
For a night and a day.
Your sweet, incurious eyes
Would widen in sharp surprise
If you knew how, under my breath,
I pray: "Let me sleep to death!
O God, let me never go home!"
But I speak through the fragrant gloom
Of your hushed and decorous room:
"Yes, I am glad I have come."

CHILDREN OF DUST

Miranda's lover sees himself
  A shield about her tender form;
He sees Miranda as a thing
  Too frail to brave a storm.
Miranda sees herself the stone
  Securely settled at his heart:
Were not his fibres woven there
  His body and soul would fly apart.

I see them both as gentle wraiths
  Blown by the wind—so dry, so light!
Their souls like fireflies in the dark
  Are piteously small and bright.
They are the victims of the world:
  They show no terror, no surprise;
But anyone who runs may read
  Disaster in their eyes.

VICTORY

I sheath my sword. In mercy go.
  Turn back from me your hopeless eyes,
  For in them all my anger dies:
I cannot face a beaten foe.

My cause was just, the fight was sweet.
  Go from me, O mine enemy,
  Before, in shame of victory,
You find me kneeling at your feet.

PART FIVE

ONE SHALL BE TAKEN AND THE OTHER LEFT

There is no Rachel any more
  And so it does not really matter.
    Leah alone is left, and she
    Goes her own way inscrutably.
  Soft-eyed she goes, content to scatter
Fine sand along a barren shore
Where there was sand enough before:
  Or from a well that has no water
    Raising a futile pitcher up
    Lifts to her lips an empty cup.
  Now she is Laban's only daughter:
There is no Rachel any more.

THE POOR KING'S DAUGHTER

Had I been bred to spinning
I might have spun
From the cold break of day
To the night's beginning.
For my own slow weaving
I might have spun a thread
Fit for the robe of a king's daughter
Or a shroud to wind the dead.

But now my hands are idle.
Idly I go
With flamboys borne before me
To dance at birth or bridal.
And it takes twelve maidens
To robe me for my sleep,
And fifty gallant gentlemen
To guard my empty keep.

VIGILS

Once I knelt in my shining mail
  Here by Thine altar all the night.
My heart beat proudly, my prayer rose loudly,
  But I looked to my armour to win the fight.

God, my lance was a broken reed,
  My mace a toy for a child's delight.
My helm is battered, my shield is shattered,
  I am stiff with wounds, and I lost the fight.

Low I kneel through the night again,
  Hear my prayer, if my prayer be right!
Take for Thy token my proud heart broken.
  God, guide my arm! I go back to the fight.

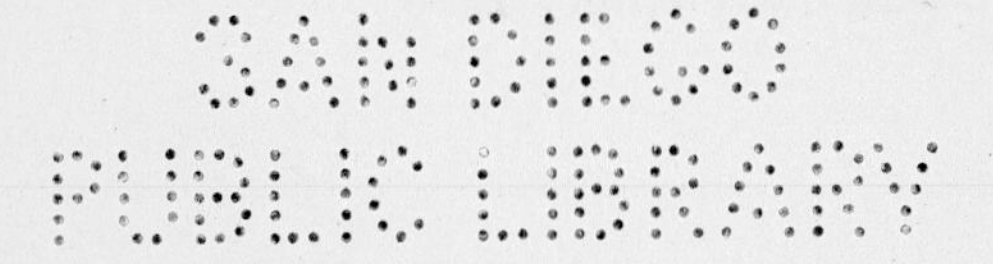

THE GIFT

He has taken away the things that I loved best
Love and youth and the harp that knew my hand.
Laughter alone is left of all the rest.
Does He mean that I may fill my days with laughter,
Or will it, too, slip through my fingers like spilt sand?

Why should I beat my wings like a bird in a net,
When I can be still and laugh at my own desire?
The wise may shake their heads at me, but yet
I should be sad without my little laughter.
The crackling of thorns is not so bad a fire.

Will He take away even the thorns from under the pot,
And send me cold and supperless to bed?
He has been good to me. I know He will not.
He gave me to keep a little foolish laughter.
I shall not lose it even when I am dead.

SANCTUARY

God has builded a house with a low lintel,
And in it He has put all manner of things.
Follow the clue through the mazes that lead to His door,
Look in! look in! see what is there for our finding.
Peace is there like a pearl, and rest and the end of seeking;
Light is there and refreshment, but there shall be more.
There we shall find for our use wide beautiful wings,
Ecstasy, solitude, space. And for those who have been too lonely
The love of friends, the warmth of a homely fire.
O never grieve again for the piteous ending
Of loveliness that could not be made to last!
There all bright passing beauty is held forever,
Free from the sense of tears, to be loved without regret.
There we shall find at their source music and love and laughter,
Colour and subtle fragrance and soft incredible textures:
Be sure we shall find what our weary hearts desire.
If we are tired of light there shall be velvet darkness

Falling across long fields, with stars, and a low voice
calling,
Calling at last the word we thought would never be
spoken.

But we, being hard and foolish and proud and mortal,
Are slow to bend and enter that humble portal.

THE END